THE AMAZING UNIVERSE

LAUREN KUKLA

Checkerboard Library

An Imprint of Abdo Publishing
abdopublishing.com

abdopublishing.com

Published by Abdo Publishing, a division of ABDO, PO Box 398166, Minneapolis, Minnesota 55439.
Printed in the United States of America, North Mankato, Minnesota
102016
012017

Design: Emily O'Malley, Mighty Media, Inc.
Production: Mighty Media, Inc.
Editor: Paige Polinsky
Cover Photograph: NASA
Interior Photographs: AP Images, p. 23 (top); Mighty Media, Inc. pp. 10, 11; NASA, pp. 13, 15, 16, 22, 23 (bottom), 25, 28; Shutterstock, pp. 5, 7, 9, 19, 27; Wikimedia Commons, p. 20

Publisher's Cataloging-in-Publication Data

Names: Kukla, Lauren, author.
Title: The amazing universe / by Lauren Kukla.
Description: Minneapolis, MN : Abdo Publishing, 2017. | Series: Exploring our universe | Includes bibliographical references and index.
Identifiers: LCCN 2016944830 | ISBN 9781680784022 (lib. bdg.) | ISBN 9781680797558 (ebook)
Subjects: LCSH: Cosmology--Juvenile literature. | Solar system--Juvenile literature. | Galaxies--Juvenile literature. | Universe--Juvenile literature.
Classification: DDC 523.1--dc23
LC record available at http://lccn.loc.gov/2016944830

CONTENTS

MISSION
EXPLORING THE COSMOS

Have you ever looked up at the night sky? You might see 2,000 stars. You could also see the moon, planets, and **satellites**. All of these belong to the universe, or cosmos. But they only make up a tiny portion of it!

Mysterious Universe

The universe is enormous. It holds billions of **galaxies** and **trillions** of stars. It is also home to mysterious **phenomena** scientists are still trying to comprehend. Scientists are just beginning to understand black holes, dark matter, and other celestial mysteries.

Understanding the Cosmos

The universe's massive size makes it hard to study. But scientists are trying to unlock its secrets. They hope

The Milky Way is our home galaxy. On a clear night with little light pollution, it can be seen from Earth.

to understand how the universe formed. Scientists are also looking at how it grew and changed. They hope this will provide clues on how and if the universe could end someday far in the future.

CHAPTER 1

THE MASSIVE UNIVERSE

The universe is a mysterious place. It contains everything that exists. This includes space, matter, energy, and time. No one knows exactly when the universe began. But many scientists believe it is about 14 billion years old. No one knows how big the universe is, either. However, scientists have found evidence that the universe is constantly expanding.

Scientists also don't know the shape of the universe for certain. Most believe it is flat. However, some scientists believe the universe curves outward, like a balloon. And others believe it curves inward, like a saddle seat.

DID YOU KNOW?

The only known universe is the one we live in. But some scientists believe that there are many different universes.

Astronomers believe there are 10 billion galaxies in the observable universe. They could hold trillions of stars!

The part of the universe we can study is **spherical**. This **sphere** is known as the observable universe. It contains all the light that has had time to reach us. We cannot see beyond this region. Scientists believe it may be 93 billion **light-years** wide. Earth sits in the center of the observable universe.

CHAPTER 2

BANG!

No one knows how the universe began. But today, most scientists accept the big bang theory. This idea suggests that all matter and energy was once contained in a single point. This point is called a singularity. It was infinitely hot and **dense**.

For some reason, the point began expanding. It expanded very quickly and then began cooling. At first, the young universe was full of tiny particles. These particles included **quarks** and electrons.

The particles were so closely packed that no light could travel through them. As the universe cooled, gravity made the quarks clump together. These clumps became protons and neutrons.

Most of the stars and galaxies we see today formed billions of years after the big bang.

UNIVERSE TIMELINE

At just one second old, the universe was already larger than our solar system. At 200 seconds old, tiny protons and neutrons began to clump together. After 380,000 years, electrons began orbiting these clumps. This formed the first atoms.

Light now traveled across the universe for the first time. It took the form of **light waves** called microwaves. The universe continued expanding, even faster than before. 300 million years after the big bang, the first stars formed.

MILKY WAY FORMS
12.6 billion years ago

OUR SOLAR SYSTEM FORMS
4.6 billion years ago

LIFE ON EARTH BEGINS
3.8 billion years ago

The first stars burned for a few million years. When they died, they exploded in brilliant supernovae. This released gas and dust into the universe. Nearly all existing elements come from the first supernovae. These elements formed more stars, planets, water, and even living things.

DID YOU KNOW?

At 15 million years old, the universe was the temperature of a sunny summer day on Earth. Some scientists believe alien life may have formed at this time.

CHAPTER 3

MYSTERIOUS MATTER

Hold your hand in front of your face. The matter forming that hand existed when the universe first began! However, it has changed its properties since then. Small particles combined to form larger particles. These larger particles eventually formed elements.

Matter is anything with mass. This means it takes up space and is affected by gravity. Matter can exist as a solid, liquid, gas, or **plasma**. It can make up very large objects, such as moons and planets. It can also make up particles so tiny we can barely detect them.

For centuries, scientists thought all matter contained the same types of particles

DID YOU KNOW?

Right now, **quarks** are the smallest known matter particles. Scientists study them with a powerful machine called an **accelerator**.

Scientists believe a large ring of dark matter surrounds galaxy cluster CL0024+17. The ring may span five million light-years.

found on Earth. They also thought stars contained most of the universe's matter. Now, scientists think most matter is invisible. They call this dark matter. Nobody knows what creates it. But its gravitational pull affects visible matter.

CHAPTER 4

BLACK HOLES

Some of the universe's most powerful objects are invisible. Black holes are extremely **dense** objects. The denser an object is, the more mass it has. And therefore, the stronger its gravitational pull.

There are two types of black holes. Stellar black holes are between 10 and 24 times as massive as the sun. Supermassive black holes are larger. They are millions of times as massive as the sun! Scientists believe there is a supermassive black hole at the center of each **galaxy**.

A black hole's gravity is extremely intense. Not even light can escape its pull! It may also eat, or pull in, gas or nearby stars. As a black hole draws in matter, it expands.

The nearest black hole is at the center of our galaxy, the Milky Way. This black hole is about 27,000 **light-years** away from Earth. Black holes may exist within other

An artist's illustration of a stellar black hole eating a star

galaxies too. Scientists don't know how they form. But they do understand stellar black holes.

Stellar black holes form when a massive star goes supernova. When a star dies, its matter collapses and bounces off its **core** in an explosion. This is a supernova. If the core is very **dense**, it will collapse into a black hole.

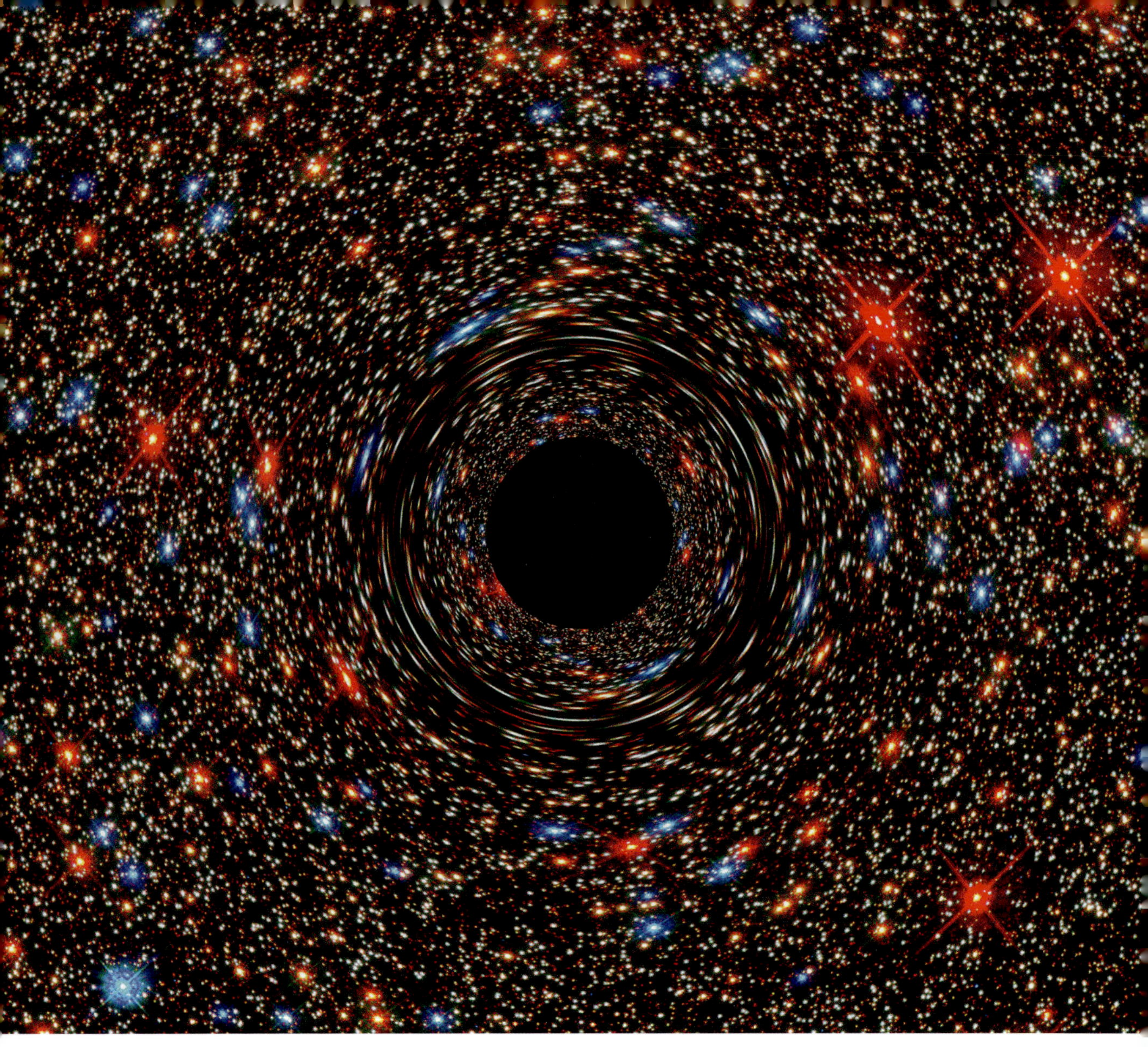

Photos captured by the Hubble Space Telescope helped create this illustration of a supermassive black hole.

What is the inside of a black hole like? No one knows for sure. But scientists have many theories. A black hole's rim is called an event horizon. Inside the event horizon is a completely dark circle. Any stars you see around the event horizon appear warped. This is because the black hole's gravity bends their light.

DID YOU KNOW?

Some scientists have theorized that black holes may be tunnels, or wormholes. These wormholes could lead to other places or times in our universe!

You would not want to explore a stellar black hole. At first, you would slowly rotate around the event horizon. But as its gravity pulled you in, you would orbit faster. The black hole's gravity would soon stretch your body apart like a long noodle. Scientists call this spaghettification.

You could cross a supermassive black hole's event horizon **intact**. But your journey wouldn't last long. Once inside, its gravity would crush you into a singularity. You would become part of the black hole!

THE END?

Scientists have taken great steps to understand how the universe began. Meanwhile, the future of the universe is still a mystery. But scientists have two main theories.

THE BIG FREEZE

In 1998, scientists made a surprising discovery. The universe's expansion is speeding up. Scientists aren't sure what force is causing this. They call it dark energy. If expansion continues, all stars and **galaxies** will eventually fly apart. Over **trillions** of years, all matter will decay. No new stars will form. The universe will be a dark, cold, empty place.

THE BIG CRUNCH

Scientists don't know if the universe will expand forever. It is possible the expansion will slow down. Then, gravity could cause the universe to **condense** back together. If that happens, the universe will collapse into a singularity. This would be like a reverse big bang. It's even possible that another big bang could occur from this point!

If a big freeze occurs, the sky will appear to be completely dark.

CHAPTER 6

STUDYING THE COSMOS

People have tried to understand the universe for thousands of years. Ancient humans used stars to navigate and measure the seasons. In the 1600s, astronomers began using telescopes to discover new planets, asteroids, and comets. The universe seemed infinite.

But in the 1820s, German astronomer Wilhelm Olbers proposed something new. He argued that the universe must have a boundary. Olbers believed that if the star-filled

Albert Einstein's ideas helped scientists make sense of the universe.

universe was infinite, the night sky would be very bright from the endless stars' light. Instead, it is mostly dark. Thus, the universe must be finite.

Almost a century later, German-American **physicist** Albert Einstein developed the theory of general relativity. This theory proved that space and time were connected. It also stated that extremely massive objects can bend space and time around them.

German astronomer Karl Schwarzschild studied Einstein's work. And in 1916, he created the first black hole theory. In 1971, scientists found a strange object in the constellation Cygnus. The object emitted strong **X-rays**. Astronomers had found the first black hole. They called the object Cygnus X-1. Three years later, astronomers found a black hole at the center of our own **galaxy**.

DID YOU KNOW?

Einstein's theories helped prove the existence of black holes. But he believed they were too strange to actually exist.

The Hubble Space Telescope was launched in 1990. Since then, it has made more than 1.2 million observations.

While some scientists searched for black holes, others were looking for clues as to how the universe formed. From the 1920s to the 1940s, scientists developed the big bang theory. Meanwhile, in 1929, US astronomer Edwin Hubble made a discovery. The farther away **galaxies** were from Earth, the faster they moved away from one another. This proved that the universe was expanding.

DID YOU KNOW?

Hubble helped discover dark matter. Scientists don't know where dark matter comes from. But it makes up about 80 percent of our universe!

SUPER SCIENTIST

FRITZ ZWICKY

In the 1930s, Swiss-American astronomer Fritz Zwicky began studying expansion. He realized one galaxy cluster's stars were moving very quickly. In fact, they were moving too fast for their gravity pull to keep the cluster together.

Zwicky theorized that an invisible matter held the cluster together. He called this force dark matter. For many years, astronomers refused to accept Zwicky's ideas. Then, in the 1970s, astronomers proved Zwicky's theory was correct. Dark matter was real!

Fritz Zwicky discovered 129 supernovae over his career.

CHAPTER 7

COSMIC CLUES

The universe is a large, mysterious place. Most of the ideas about its beginning and ending are just theories. Scientists have never seen dark matter or a black hole. Many of their ideas are based on cosmic clues.

Radiation is an important clue. Radiation is energy given off by something. This energy can take the form of visible light. But some types of energy are invisible. This includes **X-ray** radiation. Special telescopes are able to measure this energy.

Black holes don't emit visible light. Scientists find them by studying the energy emitted by nearby stars. As a star orbits a black hole, its gas shell is drawn toward the black hole. This gas spirals around the event horizon. As the gas spirals, it gets very hot. Eventually, it emits large amounts of radio waves and X-rays.

X-ray radiation given off by a distant galaxy

DID YOU KNOW?

Cosmic radiation is everywhere in the universe. It's even in your television set! About 1% of television **static** is caused by light created by the big bang.

Radiation also provides clues to the big bang. Right after the big bang, the universe was extremely hot. As it cooled, it left behind microwave radiation. This radiation is just a few degrees above **absolute zero**. It cannot be seen with the naked eye. But scientists can find it using special telescopes.

Scientists will continue to look for cosmic clues. They will try to discover how the universe began and ended. We may never know the answers. But scientists will keep trying to understand black holes, dark matter, and other mysteries of our amazing universe.

TOOLS OF DISCOVERY

LARGE HADRON COLLIDER

The Large Hadron Collider (LHC) was designed to replicate the conditions of the big bang. Built in 2008, the machine sits on the border of France and Switzerland. It is in an underground tunnel that is 17 miles (27 km) long.

The LHC accelerates particles to high speeds. Then, scientists wait for the particles to collide. Scientists hope this will demonstrate how the big bang happened. The LHC may also teach them about dark matter and dark energy. What scientists discover could change the laws of physics.

An illustration of the inside of the LHC

BLACK HOLE GUIDEBOOK

Stellar Mass Black Holes

- Location: Anywhere in the universe where stars are found
- Formation: Form when an extremely massive star dies in a supernova
- Size: 10 to 24 times more massive than our sun
- Nearest Stellar Mass Black Hole: V4641 Sgr
  - » Location: Sagittarius constellation
  - » Distance from Earth: 1,600 **light-years**
  - » Date of Discovery: 1999

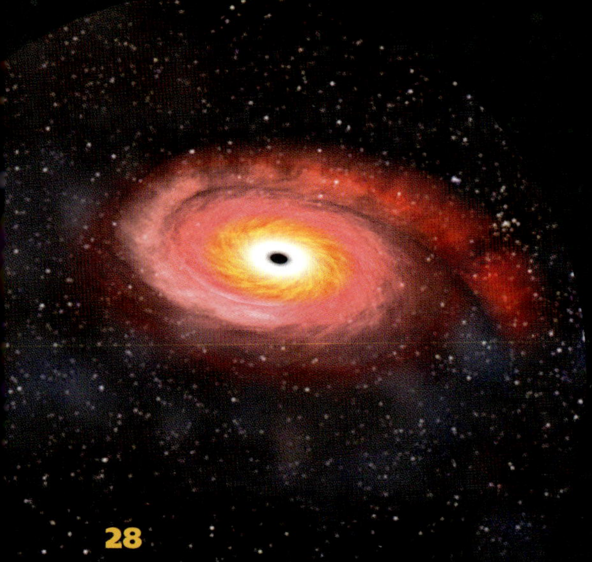

An illustration of a black hole swallowing a neutron star. Neutron stars are the smallest and densest stars in the universe.

Supermassive Black Holes

- Location: Typically found at the center of **galaxies**
- Formation: Unknown
- Size: 1 million to 21 billion times more massive than our sun
- Nearest Supermassive Black Hole: Sagittarius A*
  - » Location: Center of the Milky Way galaxy
  - » Distance from Earth: 2,600 **light-years**
  - » Date of Discovery: 1974

DID YOU KNOW?

In 2005, scientists discovered the most powerful explosion in the universe. It was caused by a supermassive black hole. The eruption has lasted more than 100 million years!

GLOSSARY

absolute zero — the temperature that is believed to be the lowest possible temperature.

accelerate — to move faster or gain speed. An accelerator is a machine that causes particles to move at very high speeds.

collide — to come together with force.

condense — to make more compact.

core — the central part of a celestial body, usually having different physical properties from the surrounding parts.

dense — thick or compact.

galaxy — a very large group of stars and planets.

intact — not broken or damaged.

light wave — an amount of light energy that travels through air or water in the shape of a wave. A wavelength is the distance between one point on a wave and the next.

light-year — the distance that light travels in one year.

phenomena (fih-NAH-muh-nuh) — facts or events that are rare or extraordinary.

physics — a science that studies matter and energy and how they interact. A physicist is a person who studies physics.

plasma — a substance that is similar to a gas but that can carry electricity.

quark — in physics, any of several particles that are believed to come in pairs. A quark is smaller than an atom.

satellite — an object, either natural or manufactured, that orbits a larger heavenly body. A manufactured satellite relays scientific information back to Earth.

sphere (SFIHR) — a globe-shaped body. Something having a globe-shaped body is spherical.

static — electrical discharges in the air that interfere with radio or television signals and cause a hissing, crackling sound.

trillion — the number 1,000,000,000,000, or one thousand billion.

X-ray — an invisible and powerful light wave that can pass through solid objects.

WEBSITES

To learn more about Exploring Our Universe, visit booklinks.abdopublishing.com. These links are routinely monitored and updated to provide the most current information available.

INDEX